CELEB★★

MOVIE STAR

CLARE HIBBERT

SEA-TO-SEA
Mankato Collingwood London

This edition first published in 2012 by

Sea-to-Sea Publications
Distributed by Black Rabbit Books
P.O. Box 3263, Mankato, Minnesota 56002

Printed in China

9 8 7 6 5 4 3 2

Published by arrangement with the
Watts Publishing Group Ltd, London.

A CIP catalog record for this book
is available from the Library of Congress.

ISBN: 978-1-59771-332-0

Planning and production by Discovery Books Limited
Managing editor: Laura Durman
Editor: Clare Hibbert
Designer: D.R. ink
Picture research: Tamsin Osler
Thanks to Lauren Ferguson and Danielle Huson

Photo acknowledgements: Corbis: pp 5 (Neal Preston), 19 (Francois Duhamel/Dreamworks/ Bureau LA Collection), 24 (Armando Gallo/Retna Ltd), 25 (Katy Winn); Getty Images: cover (George Pimentel/WireImage), pp 1 and 20 (Martin Bureau/AFP), 6 (Barry King/FilmMagic), 7 (James Devaney/WireImage), 13 (Sean Gallup), 14–15 (Leon Neal/AFP), 16 (Bobby Bank/ WireImage), 18, 21 (Patrick Lin/AFP), 27 (John Lazar/WireImage), 28–29 (Kevin Mazur/ WireImage); Rex Features: pp 4–5 (Sony Pics/Everett), 8–9 (Paramount/Everett), 10 (New Line/Everett), 11 (Geoff Robinson), 12 and 31 (MGM/Everett), 15, 16–17 (Paramount/ Everett), 22–23 (Disney Channel/Everett); Shutterstock Images: p 3 (cvijovic zarko).

Every attempt has been made to clear copyright. Should there be any inadvertent omission, please apply to the Publishers for rectification.

To the best of its knowledge, the Publisher believes the facts in this book to be true at the time of going to press. However, due to the nature of celebrity, it is impossible to guarantee that all the facts will still be current at the time of reading.

February 2011
RD/6000006415/001

CONTENTS

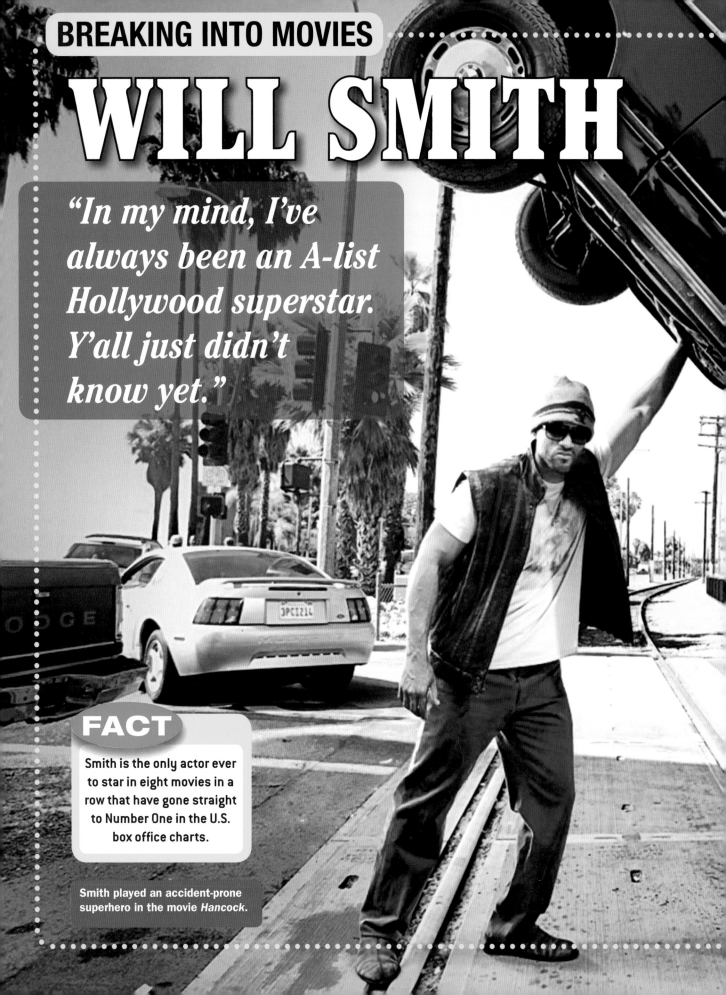

WILL SMITH

> *"In my mind, I've always been an A-list Hollywood superstar. Y'all just didn't know yet."*

FACT

Smith is the only actor ever to star in eight movies in a row that have gone straight to Number One in the U.S. box office charts.

Smith played an accident-prone superhero in the movie *Hancock*.

Smith made his acting name in the sitcom *The Fresh Prince of Bel Air*.

Since the days of the very first silent movies, audiences have adored movie stars. Today, big-name actors like Will Smith have millions of fans. Stars of the so-called silver screen are the ultimate celebrities.

The Movie Industry

Movies are made everywhere, but Hollywood, California is the movie capital of the world. This was where the first "talkies" (movies with sound) were made in the 1920s. Thousands of young hopefuls arrive in Hollywood every year.

The Fresh Prince

Very few movie actors just come out of nowhere. African-American actor Will Smith was a rapper after leaving high school. From the mid-1980s to the mid-1990s he performed as a vocalist alongside DJ Jazzy Jeff, under the name the Fresh Prince. The duo's "Parents Just Don't Understand" won the first Grammy for a hip-hop record ever.

From Music to TV

Inspired by the "Parents Just Don't Understand" video, U.S. TV channel NBC offered Smith the lead in a sitcom, *The Fresh Prince of Bel Air*. The show ran from 1990 to 1996 and earned Smith two Golden Globe nominations.

Making Movies

Like many stars, Smith was offered movie work because he was a success on TV. He appeared in a couple of movies before his breakthrough role in *Independence Day* (1996). Since then, he has won two Oscar nominations for *Ali* and *The Pursuit of Happyness*. He's built a career as a leading man, and has also made music as a solo artist.

CELEB BIO

Date of birth **September 25, 1968**

Place of birth **West Philadelphia, Pennsylvania**

Key movies *Independence Day* (1996), *Men in Black* (1997), *Ali* (2001), *I, Robot* (2004), *The Pursuit of Happyness* (2006), *Hancock* (2008)

Achievements **Multiple Grammy Awards; nominations for four Golden Globes and two Academy Awards (Oscars)**

Check out Will Smith's official web site **www.willsmith.com**

ANGELINA JOLIE

Movie stars come from all sorts of backgrounds. Some are just one- or two-hit wonders, but what about megastars like Angelina Jolie? The actors who have long, successful careers really work at it, studying new techniques that will help them make the most of their natural talent.

Jolie with partner Brad Pitt at a movie premiere.

Acting Schools

Many successful stars took acting lessons as children, and some attended drama schools. World-famous actress Angelina Jolie went to the Lee Strasberg Institute in New York. Other famous schools include the New York Film Academy and the American Conservatory Theater in the United States, and RADA and Italia Conti in the UK.

Method Acting

Jolie attended Lee Strasberg because her mother, Marcheline Bertrand, had studied there. Other former pupils include Julianne Moore, Adam Sandler, and Julia Roberts. The institute teaches method acting—where actors use real experiences of their own to help them identify with and portray a character as convincingly as possible.

A Stellar Career

Both of Jolie's parents were movie actors, so she already had acting in her blood. Her first leading role in a Hollywood movie was in 1995, with *Hackers*. Four years later, she won her first Academy Award as best supporting actress for *Girl, Interrupted*.

Multitalented

Today, Jolie is recognized as an extraordinary acting talent, able to portray a gun-slinging action hero (*Lara Croft: Tomb Raider*) or a distraught mother (*Changeling*) with equal success. She has many hit movies to her name, and also provided the voices for Lola the angelfish in *Shark Tale* (2004) and Tigress in *Kung Fu Panda* (2008).

FACT

Jolie made a brief appearance in *Lookin' to Get Out* at the age of seven. The movie starred her father, Jon Voight.

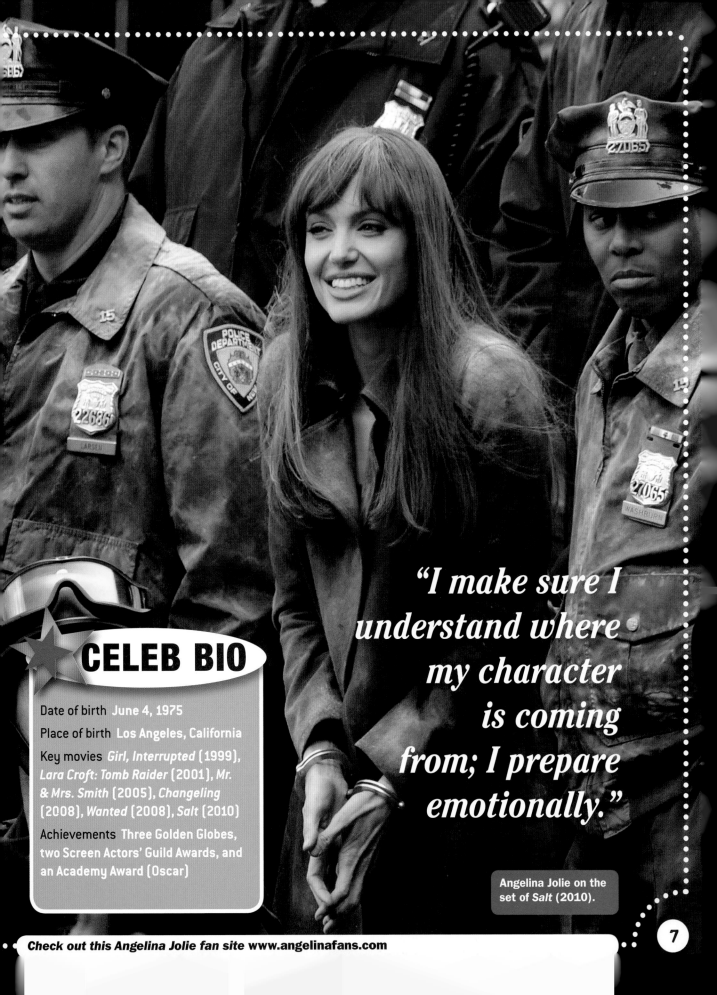

CELEB BIO

Date of birth **June 4, 1975**

Place of birth **Los Angeles, California**

Key movies *Girl, Interrupted* (1999), *Lara Croft: Tomb Raider* (2001), *Mr. & Mrs. Smith* (2005), *Changeling* (2008), *Wanted* (2008), *Salt* (2010)

Achievements **Three Golden Globes, two Screen Actors' Guild Awards, and an Academy Award (Oscar)**

"I make sure I understand where my character is coming from; I prepare emotionally."

Angelina Jolie on the set of *Salt* (2010).

Established actors rely on an agent to find them work —it leaves them free to concentrate on acting. Agents have plenty of contacts in the movie industry, so they hear about upcoming movies before anyone else. Finding a good agent is essential! Child star Freddie Highmore has one of the best in the business.

"Well, you just sort of think about what the character's thinking, and then you're in character."

FREDDIE HIGHMORE

Special Agent

Sue Latimer is Freddie Highmore's mom—and also his agent. She represents some great British talents besides Freddie, including *Harry Potter* stars Daniel Radcliffe and Imelda Staunton (who plays Dolores Umbridge).

Selecting Scripts

Latimer's job is to help Freddie and her other clients (the actors she looks after) build successful careers. She finds out which directors are making new movies and then puts forward clients for roles that will suit them. Her job involves reading lots of movie scripts, negotiating contracts—and being good at ironing out problems.

Boy Star

Freddie Highmore comes from a showbiz family. His younger brother, Bertie, played his onscreen brother in the comedy *Women Talking Dirty* (1999), while his dad, actor Edward Highmore, played his father in the TV adaptation *Jack and the Beanstalk: The Real Story* (2001). Highmore's breakthrough movie role was Peter in *Finding Neverland*, which co-starred Johnny Depp and Kate Winslet.

Screen Success

Highmore's acting and his mom's connections are a winning combination. Since *Finding Neverland*, Freddie has starred in numerous hits, including *Charlie and the Chocolate Factory* and *The Spiderwick Chronicles*.

Highmore in *The Spiderwick Chronicles*.

FACT

Highmore provided the
voices for Lyra's familiar,
Pan, in *The Golden Compass*
and for the title character
in *Astro Boy*.

DAKOTA BLUE RICHARDS

Dakota as Lyra in *The Golden Compass*.

How do actors land their roles? If moviemakers have a particular actor in mind for a specific role, they just ask their agent directly. At other times, casting directors hold auditions to find the members of the cast. That's how Dakota Blue Richards won the lead in *The Golden Compass*.

Open Auditions...

Auditions are when actors come to show off their acting skills, in the hope of being given a part. Anyone can attend open auditions. They are particularly useful when directors are looking for fresh talent, for example, someone to play a child's role.

... and Closed

Not all auditions are open. Actors have to be invited to attend a "closed" audition. This sort of audition is useful if a casting director wants an established actor for a role, but can't choose between two or three of them.

Landing Lyra

Dakota Blue Richards found out about *The Golden Compass* auditions from the children's news program, *Newsround*. She was 12 at the time. After the first audition, she was called back a second time, and then a third, before doing a screen test (being filmed performing a scene). The movie's director, Chris Weitz, said, "I didn't have any doubts about Dakota. She looks not quite tamed, and that's Lyra."

Drama Queen

Dakota had always enjoyed acting. From the age of 11 she attended a theater school for lessons in drama, musical theater, singing, jazz tap, and ballet. Even so, she never expected to star in a big-budget movie!

CELEB BIO

Date of birth **April 11, 1994**

Place of birth **London, UK**

Key movies **The Golden Compass (2007), The Secret of Moonacre (2009)**

Achievements **A Young Artist Award nomination**

"My mom said we wouldn't go [to the casting] if the weather was bad, so it's lucky it wasn't raining!"

Check out Dakota Blue Richards' web site www. dakota-richards.net

DANIEL CRAIG

★ CELEB BIO

Date of birth March 2, 1968

Place of birth Chester, Cheshire, UK

Key movies *Lara Croft: Tomb Raider* (2001), *Layer Cake* (2004), *Casino Royale* (2006), *The Golden Compass* (2007), *Quantum of Solace* (2008)

Achievements One BAFTA nomination, one Empire Award, and two British Independent Film Awards

Craig as Bond in *Quantum of Solace.*

Landing a part takes a little luck and a lot of effort—but that's only the start. Then the real work begins. Daniel Craig spent months preparing for the role of spy hero James Bond before a single second of film was actually shot.

Word Perfect

An actor's first job is to learn the script inside-out. Life is busy on set, and no one wants to waste time with someone who can't remember the lines. With the words memorized, the actor starts trying to "get inside" the character. This might involve learning a new accent or studying behavior.

Body Work

Actors often have to lose or put on weight so that they look the part. A nutritionist often plans a special diet to make sure the weight loss or gain happens safely. Daniel Craig also worked out to make his physique convincing as James Bond. He went running and cycling and pumped weights at the gym.

Bond in Action

Craig said he wanted his Bond to look "physically capable...as fit as possible." He knew his body had to be in peak condition so that he could do stunts in the movie and he didn't want anyone to criticize him for not looking the part.

"The Name's Bond"

Craig was the sixth actor to play Bond (Sean Connery, George Lazenby, Roger Moore, Timothy Dalton, and Pierce Brosnan have also played the role). Some fans weren't sure about Craig, but in the end his classy performances in *Casino Royale* and *Quantum of Solace* won wonderful reviews.

"Bond is a huge iconic figure in movie history, and those things don't come along very often."

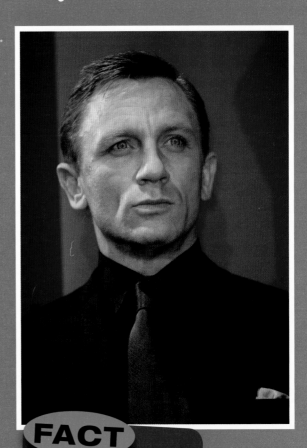

FACT

All kinds of accidents took place during the shooting of *Quantum of Solace*, including Craig slicing off the top of one of his fingers!

Grint (left), Watson (center), and Radcliffe (right) attending the premiere of *Harry Potter and the Half-Blood Prince*.

DANIEL RADCLIFFE, EMMA WATSON & RUPERT GRINT

Shooting a movie can take months. For the actors and everyone else involved, this means being away from family and friends. For child actors, there is the added difficulty of missing school.

The *Harry Potter* Movies

Harry Potter and the Philosopher's Stone (2001) was the first of the eight *Harry Potter* movies. Set in a school for wizards, the movies have a huge cast of children. The three stars are Daniel Radcliffe, who plays Harry, and Rupert Grint and Emma Watson, who play his friends, Ron and Hermione.

Studios and Locations

Radcliffe, Grint, and Watson were just 11, 12, and 10 at the time of the first movie. The three grew up together on set, like brothers and sister. The filming took place at Leavesden Film Studios, Hertfordshire, UK, on sets built in converted aircraft hangars, and on location. Alnwick Castle in Northumberland was the main location used for Hogwart's School.

Filming Family

During filming, all the cast and crew become one big family, or "tribe" as Radcliffe once put it. Working and socializing together every day is intense—but it forges deep friendships. When the actors were still school age, private tutors helped them keep up with their studies, and they went back to their respective schools during the short breaks between movies.

CELEB BIO

Dates of birth Daniel Radcliffe July 23, 1989, Emma Watson April 15, 1990, Rupert Grint August 24, 1988

Places of birth London, UK (Daniel), Paris, France (Emma), Hertfordshire, UK (Rupert)

Key movies All eight *Harry Potter* movies (2001–2011)

Achievements Joint nominations for an MTV Movie Award, an Empire Award, and two Young Artist Awards, as well as individual awards and nominations

Grint on the set of *Harry Potter and the Deathly Hallows*.

"I'm glad that we have each other. I would have been so lonely if it was just about one kid." EMMA WATSON

SHIA LABEOUF

The most exciting movies feature daring stunts. Characters race across rooftops, dangle from helicopters, and perform other extraordinary feats. Often, these are the work of stunt artists, though American actor Shia LaBeouf does many of his own stunts.

Stunt doubles for Harrison Ford (left) and Shia LaBeouf (right) perform a motorcycle chase for *Indiana Jones and the Kingdom of the Crystal Skull*.

All in a Day's Work

Stunt artists are people whose job is to stand in for actors when their character has to do something dangerous. Some have their own areas of specialization, such as escaping from fires, riding horses, fighting, or taking part in car chases. Most stuntmen and women are trained in gymnastics or martial arts or both.

The Real Thing

When a stunt double is involved, the scene has to be shot carefully so viewers don't see the stunt artist's face. When actors perform their own stunts, the action is more believable because we can see the actors' expressions. Shia LaBeouf did all his own stunts in *Transformers* (2007).

Action Hero

Playing Mutt Williams in *Indiana Jones and the Kingdom of the Crystal Skull* gave LaBeouf more opportunities for stuntwork, but he had a double for the most dangerous scenes—like when Mutt leaps between jeeps during a high-speed chase. For *Transformers: Revenge of the Fallen*, LaBeouf used a double for some stunts but still suffered a couple of injuries—first a broken hand, and then a spike through his eye. He was lucky not to lose his sight.

Top Teen

LaBeouf's breakthrough movie role was Stanley Yelnats IV in the family mystery *Holes* (2003). Just 17 years old, he'd already been acting in television for five years, and had won a Daytime Emmy for playing Steven in the Disney Channel series, *Even Stevens*.

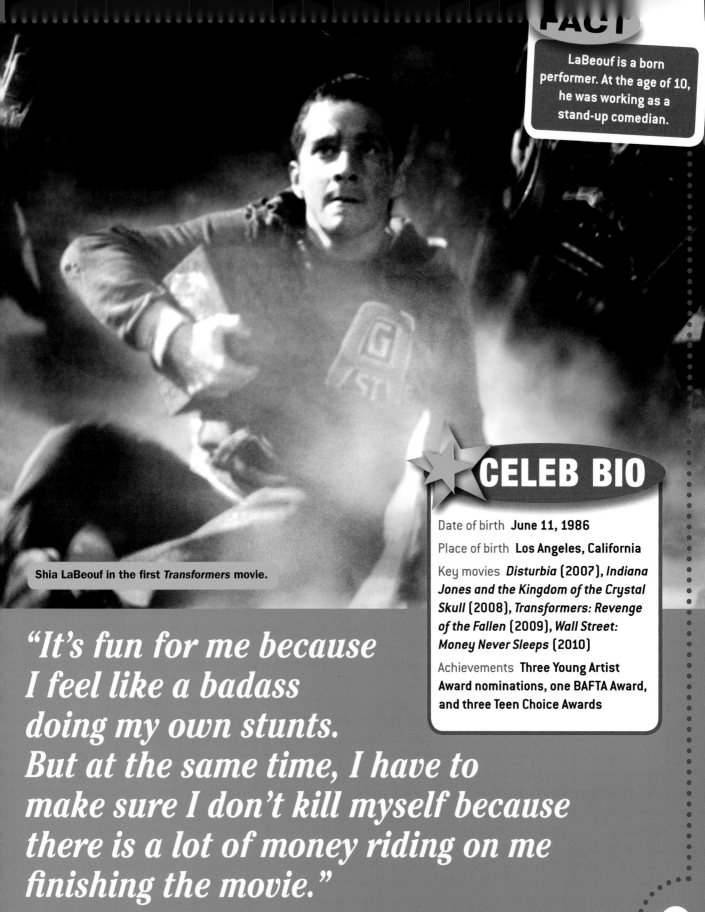

Shia LaBeouf in the first *Transformers* movie.

★ CELEB BIO

Date of birth **June 11, 1986**

Place of birth **Los Angeles, California**

Key movies **Disturbia** (2007), *Indiana Jones and the Kingdom of the Crystal Skull* (2008), *Transformers: Revenge of the Fallen* (2009), *Wall Street: Money Never Sleeps* (2010)

Achievements **Three Young Artist Award nominations, one BAFTA Award, and three Teen Choice Awards**

"It's fun for me because I feel like a badass doing my own stunts. But at the same time, I have to make sure I don't kill myself because there is a lot of money riding on me finishing the movie."

"I absolutely want to have a career where you make 'em laugh and make 'em cry. It's all theater."

JIM CARREY

Family movies are motion pictures that appeal to all ages. In the U.S., that means movies that have been rated "G." Viewers young and old can be sure that there won't be anything too terrifying—or too embarrassing—to watch.

A Fine Line

Moviemakers have to consider the ratings when they make and edit movies. If a movie is aimed at children, it can't contain really scary scenes. Canadian star Jim Carrey is brilliant at treading that fine line—thrilling young audiences, but not terrifying them!

Funny Face

Carrey's background was stand-up comedy. He was a movie actor for more than a decade before landing the lead in the 1994 blockbuster, *Ace Ventura: Pet Detective*. It was his 14th movie! Carrey became famous for his impressive range of silly voices and facial expressions. *The Mask* made the most of his "rubber" features, turning him into a comic-book-style superhero whose face could stretch and s-t-r-e-t-c-h.

In Costume

Carrey's starred in many family movies—although sometimes he's hard to recognize. He turned green in 2000 to play the Grinch in *How the Grinch Stole Christmas* and aged with the help of some makeup to play villainous Count

Olaf in 2004's *Lemony Snicket's A Series of Unfortunate Events*. In 2009, in *A Christmas Carol*, he managed to play four roles—Scrooge and all three of the ghosts.

Carrey as the Christmas-hating Grinch, who forces his pet dog to be a reindeer.

FACT

Two of Carrey's movies, *How the Grinch Stole Christmas* (2000) and *Horton Hears a Who!* (2008), are based on Dr. Seuss books.

Carrey in *Lemony Snicket* with Meryl Streep as Aunt Josephine.

⭐ CELEB BIO

Date of birth January 17, 1962

Place of birth Newmarket, Ontario, Canada

Key movies *Ace Ventura: Pet Detective* (1994), *The Mask* (1994), *The Cable Guy* (1996), *Bruce Almighty* (2003), *Lemony Snicket's A Series of Unfortunate Events* (2004), *A Christmas Carol* (2009)

Achievements Two Golden Globe Awards and a BAFTA nomination

FACT

Before landing the lead female role in *The Mask*, Diaz worked for five years as a fashion model. She was signed to top modeling agency, Elite.

CAMERON DIAZ

It might seem odd for animation-makers to pay big money just for a voice—but the right star can make all the difference. That's why famous movie stars like Cameron Diaz can often be heard in cartoons and animations, even if they do not exactly *appear* in them!

All About Looks

Sometimes, animators draw or design the character so that he, she, or it resembles the actor speaking the part. The blonde giant Ginormica in *Monsters vs. Aliens*, for example, looks quite a lot like Reese Witherspoon, who provided the voice.

Ogre Princess

Red-haired Princess Fiona in the *Shrek* movies doesn't really resemble Cameron Diaz, though, whether she's in ogre or pretty princess mode! Diaz provides Princess Fiona's talking voice, but not the singing. The first *Shrek* movie came out in 2001 and the fifth and last is due for release in 2013.

Model Background

Diaz hit the big screen in 1994 when she landed the part of Tina Carlyle in *The Mask*. She had no acting experience, and won the part on the strength of her looks and natural talent.

Star Quality

After *The Mask*, Diaz took acting lessons and appeared in several low-budget movies. In 1997, she starred in *My Best Friend's Wedding* and *A Life Less Ordinary*—and she has never looked back. Being chosen to play Natalie in the *Charlie's Angels* movies confirmed her top star status. Diaz's acting has earned her nominations for numerous awards, and she has her own star on the Hollywood Walk of Fame.

Diaz with her alter ego, the ogre Princess Fiona.

CELEB BIO

Date of birth **August 30, 1972**

Place of birth **San Diego, California**

Key movies ***There's Something about Mary* (1998), *Charlie's Angels* (2000), *Shrek* (2001), *Gangs of New York* (2002), *My Sister's Keeper* (2009), *Knight and Day* (2010)**

Achievements **Four Golden Globe nominations and one BAFTA nomination**

"Acting allows me to tell a lot of stories —you know, start at the beginning, finish at the end, and tell everything in between."

ZAC EFRON & VANESSA HUDGENS

Appearing in a musical presents its own challenges. Being a skillful actor is not enough—you also need to be able to sing and dance. The young stars of *High School Musical (HSM)* sparkle with talent and energy.

Popular Appeal

Musicals have always been popular. Moviegoers find the combination of music, dance, and—usually—humor tremendously uplifting. Even so, the *HSM* movies have surprised everyone with their amazing box office success.

Disney Hits

The first two *HSM*s were made for television and shown on the Disney Channel. They were so popular that *HSM*3 was released in movie theaters. It made $80 million in its first weekend! The two leading stars, Zac Efron and Vanessa Hudgens, are boyfriend and girlfriend on screen and off. Efron plays basketball captain Troy Bolton and Hudgens plays multitalented girl genius Gabriella Montez.

Leading Boy…

Efron started acting lessons age 11 and later studied singing, too. Starting in 2002 he guest-starred on various TV shows, from *The Suite Life of Zack & Cody* to *CSI: Miami*. Playing Troy in *HSM* made him a teen heartthrob, and he's since appeared in the movies *Hairspray*, *17 Again*, and *Me and Orson Welles*.

… & Leading Girl

Hudgens appeared in local musicals from the age of eight. Like Efron, she appeared on TV before *HSM*. She also pursued a career as a singer —her debut album *V* came out in 2006 and *Identified* followed in 2008. Hudgens won praise for her acting and singing in *Bandslam in 2009* and she went on to star in the fantasy movie, *Beastly*.

Performing in *HSM*, from left: Corbin Bleu, Zac Efron, Chris Warren Jr., and Vanessa Hudgens.

CELEB BIO

Dates of birth **Zac Efron October 18, 1987, Vanessa Hudgens December 14, 1988**

Place of birth **California**

Key movies **High School Musical (2006), High School Musical 2 (2007), High School Musical 3: Senior Year (2008)**

Achievements **Joint nominations for an MTV Movie Award and a Teen Choice Award and one joint win of a Teen Choice Award**

"*As an audience member, I know the feeling I have when I leave a musical is unrivaled...*" ZAC EFRON

Robert Pattinson photographed to promote *New Moon*, the second movie in the *Twilight* series.

ROBERT PATTINSON

"I didn't want to do a stupid teen movie...I didn't want to be involved in something just to make money."

The movie industry sometimes takes risks, but the big picture companies prefer to invest in movies that are guaranteed to be a success. Once they hit on a winning formula, they like to repeat that in sequels and prequels.

Twilight

Movies adapted from best-selling book series are highly popular with Hollywood. Stephenie Meyer's *Twilight* novels are the perfect example. The movie adaptations began with *Twilight* (2008), *New Moon* (2009), and *Eclipse* (2010), all starring Robert Pattinson as the vampire hero, Edward Cullen. Pattinson had already appeared as schoolboy wizard Cedric Diggory in two of the *Harry Potter* movies.

Pros and Cons

Landing a starring role in a series of movies can be a mixed blessing. It guarantees the actor work for the run of series, but it can also lead to typecasting. Luckily for Pattinson, he's already been cast in very different roles. He played the artist Salvador Dalí in *Little Ashes* (2008) and a young student in the romantic drama *Remember Me* (2010).

Aging Gracefully

Sequels, especially to movies like *Twilight* that star young actors, need to be shot quickly before the stars begin to look too old for their parts. This can be tricky. The *Harry Potter* novels span the period that Harry attends Hogwart's—seven years—but the movies themselves took more than ten years to make.

Pattinson signing autographs for his fans.

CELEB BIO

Date of birth May 13, 1986

Place of birth London, UK

Key movies *Harry Potter and the Goblet of Fire* (2005), *Little Ashes* (2008), *Twilight* (2008), *New Moon* (2009), *Eclipse* (2010), *Breaking Dawn* (2011)

Achievements Three Teen Choice Awards and three MTV Movie Awards

Check out the official Twilight web site www.twilightthemovie.com

NICOLE KIDMAN

CELEB BIO

Date of birth **June 20, 1967**

Place of birth **Honolulu, Hawaii**

Key movies *Dead Calm* (1989), *To Die For* (1995), *Moulin Rouge!* (2001), *The Hours* (2002), *Happy Feet* (2006), *The Golden Compass* (2007), *Australia* (2008), *Rabbit Hole* (2010)

Achievements **One Academy Award (Oscar), a BAFTA, and a Golden Globe**

For any movie actor, winning an Academy Award is the ultimate accolade. Australian-American actress Nicole Kidman was thrilled to win one for her performance as writer Virginia Woolf in the 2002 movie, *The Hours*.

Academy Awards

The "Oscars," or Academy Awards, are the movie industry's most prestigious awards. They are presented by the American Academy of Motion Picture Arts and Sciences, which represents the big Hollywood movie companies. Winning categories range from best movie and best director to best makeup and best visual effects.

Best Actress

Kidman won her Academy Award for Best Actress in a Leading Role for *The Hours*. She was a runner-up in the same category for *Moulin Rouge!* Like all Oscar winners, Kidman received her statuette at a star-studded awards ceremony in Los Angeles.

Breakthrough Movie

Kidman had spent her early career on television in Australia. Then, in 1989, she appeared in the Hollywood thriller, *Dead Calm*. Kidman's convincing portrayal of a woman held captive onboard a yacht brought her international respect. In 1990, Kidman began a high-profile romance with Tom Cruise, her costar in *Days of Thunder*. Their ten-year marriage threw her into the media spotlight.

Range of Roles

Kidman's celebrity helped bring her a variety of roles, in which she was able to show off her wide-ranging talent. She has entertained audiences as a struggling, American Civil War-era farmer (*Cold Mountain*), a confused widow (*Birth*), and a comedy witch (*Bewitched*).

MOVIE AWARDS

Kidman has won or been nominated for various movie industry awards. The most important ones include:

Academy Awards Also known as the Oscars; presented by the American movie industry each February or March

AFI Awards Presented by the Australian Film Industry each December

BAFTAs Presented by the UK movie industry each February

Golden Globes Decided by international journalists living in Hollywood and presented every January

MTV Movie Awards Decided by viewers of the music channel MTV and presented each June

Kidman accepts her Oscar for *The Hours*.

"Why do you come to the Academy Awards when the world is in such turmoil [with the outbreak of the Iraq War]? Because art is important."

AT THE 2003 ACADEMY AWARDS

MILEY CYRUS

"My goal in my music and my acting is always to make people happy."

★ CELEB BIO

Date of birth **November 23, 1992**

Place of birth **Nashville, Tennessee**

Key movies *Bolt* (2008), *Hannah Montana: The Movie* (2009), *The Last Song* (2010)

Achievements **One Golden Globe nomination**

Stars of blockbuster movies have to get used to something very strange. Not only do they see their own faces everywhere on movie posters and magazine covers—their pictures also appear on all kinds of merchandise!

Licensing

Hit movies make only part of their profit through box office and DVD sales. The rest comes from soundtracks and licensed products. One of the biggest licensing success stories of recent years is the character Hannah Montana, played by Miley Cyrus. Cyrus's face has been splashed across everything from lunchboxes to T-shirts, and the movie has also spawned all sorts of spin-off books and magazines.

Hit with Hannah

Hannah Montana began life as a television series on the Disney Channel, but it was so successful that it led to a movie. The storyline centers around Miley Stewart, a seemingly ordinary high school girl, who's living a double life as a famous pop singer, Hannah Montana.

Music and More

Cyrus is living her own double life, as an actress and a singer-songwriter. Following her strong performances as Hannah Montana, she's released chart-topping albums—the series and movie soundtracks and a solo album as herself, entitled *Breakout*. She's also recorded with the Jonas Brothers and toured with The Cheetah Girls. She's even published a memoir of her life so far, called *Miles to Go*.

FACT

Cyrus's dad is a celebrity, too. He is the famous country singer, Billy Ray Cyrus.

GLOSSARY

accolade Recognition of talent or success.

agent Someone who represents actors and finds them work, for example, in movies, television programs, and stage shows.

animation A movie, sometimes called a cartoon, that shows successive still images (or computer-generated images) very quickly, so that characters appear to be moving.

audition A short performance given by an actor in order to show that he or she would be suitable for a part.

blockbuster A movie (or book) that is a great commercial success.

box office The place in a movie theater that sells tickets. When movies are described as box office flops or box office successes, it means they have sold very few tickets or lots and lots of tickets.

cast All the actors in a movie.

casting director The person in charge of finding actors to play the different roles in a movie.

contract An agreement that must be stuck to, by law.

director The person who is in charge of making a movie. His or her vision for how the movie should be guides everyone else involved.

double Someone who stands in for an actor in some scenes.

edit In movies, to cut and shape the scenes that have been shot to create a watchable movie.

established Describes an actor who has appeared in several successful movies.

Grammy An award that recognizes musical excellence, presented by the U.S. record industry.

Hollywood Walk of Fame A sidewalk in Hollywood, California, that is decorated with more than 2,000 stars, each of which features the name of a successful movie actor or character.

iconic Having special status.

licensing Making products that feature a copyrighted character, after paying a license fee to the copyright holder, for example, the movie company.

location A "real" place where scenes are shot for a movie, as opposed to a set built in a studio.

martial arts Skillful sports that originated in eastern Asia, especially Japan, as fighting or self-defense techniques, for example, judo and karate.

merchandise Goods for sale, especially products used to promote a movie.

method acting A technique used by actors to help them portray emotions and characters convincingly. Method actors draw on their own experiences to try to really identify with the roles they play.

modeling agency A company that finds work for models.

musical A movie or play that contains lots of song-and-dance routines.

negotiating Agreeing the terms or conditions of something, such as a contract.

nutritionist Someone who studies food and diets.

prequel A movie that describes events leading up to the story in an existing movie.

producer The person who works with a movie's director to organize the practicalities of making the movie happen, for example, by raising finances, putting the cast together, and booking studios.

rating The classification given to a movie by the Motion Picture Association of America, as a guide for viewers and moviemakers.

review An opinion expressed in the media about something creative, such as a movie, book, or musical performance.

screenplay The complete text of a movie, including descriptions of the sets or scenes and all of the dialogue (words spoken by the actors).

sequel A movie that continues the story from an existing movie.

set Where a movie or a scene in a movie is shot.

silver screen Another word for motion pictures, or the movie industry.

stunt A daring act that requires courage and skill.

stunt double Someone who performs stunts in place of an actor.

title character The name of a character that is also used in the title of a work. Harry Potter is the title character of *Harry Potter and the Philosopher's Stone*, for example.

typecasting When an actor is always offered the same sort of role.

UNICEF The United Nations Children's Fund, a charity that campaigns worldwide to improve children's lives.

vocalist Singer.

BOOKS

Complete Harry Potter Collection by J.K. Rowling (Bloomsbury, 2008)

Hot Celebrity Biographies: Daniel Radcliffe by Stephanie Watson (Enslow Publishers, 2009)

Livewire Real Lives: Will Smith by Julia Holt (Hodder Murray, 2005)

Modern Role Models: Angelina Jolie by Lydia Bjornlund (Mason Crest, 2009)

Robert Pattinson: True Love Never Dies by Josie Rusher (Orion, 2008)

Today's Superstars: Cameron Diaz by Geoffrey M Horn (Gareth Stevens, 2005)

DVDS

Bond Complete Collection (MGM, 2008)

Hannah Montana the Movie (Disney, 2009)

High School Musical 3: Senior Year (Disney, 2009)

WEB SITES

www.imdb.com
The Internet Movie Database is an excellent resource with information on movies and actors.

www.oscar.go.com
The official web site of the Academy Awards.

http://home.disney.go.com
The web site for information on Disney movies and TV shows, including pages on Miley Cyrus and *High School Musical*.